Lerner SPORTS

GREATEST OF ALL TIME PLAYERS

G.O.A.T. BASKETBALL
SHOOTING GUARDS

Audrey Stewart

Lerner Publications ◆ Minneapolis

SPORTS THRILLS
MEET
RESEARCH SKILLS

Lerner **SPORTS**

Free Database Trial: **lernersports.com**

Lerner Publications Company
An imprint of Lerner Publishing Group, Inc.
241 First Avenue North
Minneapolis, MN 55401 USA

For reading levels and more information, look up this title at www.lernerbooks.com.

Main body text set in Aptifer Sans LT Pro.
Typeface provided by Linotype AG.

Library of Congress Cataloging-in-Publication Data

Names: Stewart, Audrey (Children's author), author.
Title: G.O.A.T. basketball shooting guards / Audrey Stewart.
Other titles: Greatest of all time shooting guards
Description: Minneapolis, MN : Lerner Publications, [2025] | Series: Lerner sports. Greatest Of All Time players | Includes bibliographical references and index. | Audience: Ages 7–11 | Audience: Grades 2–3 | Summary: "Basketball's shooting guards do a lot more than shoot. They grab rebounds, play tough defense, and thrill fans with high-flying dunks. Meet the best shooting guards, explore their careers, and then choose your top 10"—Provided by publisher.
Identifiers: LCCN 2023043449 (print) | LCCN 2023043450 (ebook) | ISBN 9798765625781 (library binding) | ISBN 9798765628744 (paperback) | ISBN 9798765633649 (epub)
Subjects: LCSH: Guards (Basketball)—United States—Biography—Juvenile literature.
Classification: LCC GV884.A1 S74 2025 (print) | LCC GV884.A1 (ebook) | DDC 796.323092/273—dc23/eng/20231025

LC record available at https://lccn.loc.gov/2023043449
LC ebook record available at https://lccn.loc.gov/2023043450

Manufactured in the United States of America
1 – CG – 7/15/24

TABLE OF CONTENTS

BIG-TIME SCORERS

The Philadelphia 76ers and the Boston Celtics were playing Game 1 of the 2023 National Basketball Association (NBA) Eastern Conference Semifinals. It was a close game. Both teams held the lead 14 times, and the game was tied 14 times.

Boston went into halftime with a three-point lead. But the 76ers outscored the Celtics in the second half. In the last seconds of the game, shooting guard James Harden sealed the win for Philadelphia with a three-pointer. Harden scored 45 points in the 119–115 victory, tying his career record for a playoff game.

FACTS AT A GLANCE

» AN IMAGE OF MICHAEL JORDAN SLAM-DUNKING A BASKETBALL BECAME THE OFFICIAL LOGO FOR NIKE'S AIR JORDAN SHOES AND CLOTHING.

» AT 6 FEET (1.8 M) AND 165 POUNDS (74.8 KG), ALLEN IVERSON IS ONE OF THE SMALLEST SHOOTING GUARDS IN NBA HISTORY.

» KOBE BRYANT IS THE ONLY SHOOTING GUARD IN HISTORY TO SCORE AT LEAST 80 POINTS IN A GAME.

» CYNTHIA COOPER WAS THE FIRST WOMEN'S NATIONAL BASKETBALL ASSOCIATION (WNBA) PLAYER IN HISTORY TO SCORE 2,500 CAREER POINTS.

Although the 76ers lost the series to Boston, Harden helped keep his team alive for all seven games of the semifinals. In Game 4, he had 42 points, eight rebounds, nine assists, four steals, and one block. His last-second three-pointer was the game-winning shot.

A shooting guard's main job is to score. They are skilled at driving to the basket for a layup,

moving around their opponent for a jump shot, or taking a long shot for a three-pointer. They are also good at passing. Shooting guards need to catch the ball, turn, and shoot quickly. Sometimes shooting guards shoot off of the dribble. This means they shoot on the move without stopping.

Klay Thompson of the Golden State Warriors (*right*) takes a jump shot just out of reach of Celtics defender Jayson Tatum.

Shooting guards need to score points, but they must also defend the other team's best shooter. Playing tough defense is important. Like James Harden in Game 4, shooting guards do a lot of scoring and a little of everything else on the court.

Cynthia Cooper was older than most WNBA players. She was 34 when she joined the Houston Comets in 1997. It was the WNBA's first season. Before playing for Houston, Cooper played on three different teams in Europe. She also played for USA Basketball's Women's National Team at the 1988 and 1992 Olympic Games.

As soon as she joined the WNBA, Cooper began making headlines. She was the Women's Sports Foundation's Sportswoman of the Year in 1998 for team sports. She won the WNBA's Most Valuable Player (MVP) award in 1997 and 1998. Cooper led the Comets to four WNBA championships in five years. In 2000, she became the first player in WNBA history to score 2,500 career points.

Although she only played five seasons, Cooper is one of the WNBA's top 20 players of all time. After she retired from playing, she coached four different college teams. She became part of the Women's Basketball Hall of Fame in 2009 and the Naismith Memorial Basketball Hall of Fame in 2010.

CYNTHIA COOPER STATS

Points	2,601
Rebounds	403
Assists	602
Three-Pointers	239

The Phoenix Mercury picked Cappie Pondexter second overall in the 2006 WNBA Draft. A fast and fierce player, Pondexter was an All-Star in her first WNBA season. In 2009, she became the first player in WNBA history to win Player of the Week for three weeks straight.

Pondexter averaged 19.2 points per game during her four seasons with the Mercury and led them to two WNBA championships. She also played in Turkey and Russia and won seven league championships there. In 2008, Pondexter helped the USA Basketball Women's National Team win gold at the Olympic Games in Beijing, China. Fans voted Pondexter one of the WNBA's top 15 players of all time, and the WNBA picked her for their anniversary teams in 2011, 2016, and 2021. Pondexter retired from playing in 2019.

CAPPIE PONDEXTER STATS

🏀 Points	6,811
🏀 Rebounds	1,520
🏀 Assists	1,578
🏀 Three-Pointers	464

RAY ALLEN

Ray Allen grew up on US military bases in the US, England, and Germany. His family settled in South Carolina for his high school years. Allen struggled to fit in at school. But he enjoyed basketball and spent his free time working on his skills.

After playing three seasons at the University of Connecticut, the Minnesota Timberwolves picked Allen fifth overall in the

1996 NBA Draft. Minnesota traded him to the Milwaukee Bucks, where he was a three-time All-Star. He averaged 19.3 points per game over six seasons with the Bucks.

Allen then played more than four seasons with the Seattle SuperSonics before joining the Boston Celtics. He played a big role in Boston's 2008 NBA championship. He scored 19 points and grabbed nine rebounds in Game 4 of the 2008 Finals, helping the Celtics earn the biggest comeback in NBA Finals history. Allen played a total of 18 NBA seasons and was a 10-time All-Star. His 2,973 three-pointers rank second most in the NBA.

RAY ALLEN STATS

Points	24,505
Rebounds	5,272
Assists	4,361
Three-Pointers	2,973

REGGIE MILLER

Reggie Miller played all 18 of his NBA seasons with the Indiana Pacers. He was a first-round draft pick in 1987. A skilled three-point shooter, Miller ranks fourth in NBA history for three-pointers.

Miller earned the nickname the Knick Killer because of his three-point shooting against the New York Knicks. In a 1995 Eastern Conference playoffs game against the Knicks, Miller scored eight points in 8.9 seconds and led the Pacers to a 107–105 comeback victory.

Miller is a five-time All-Star and joined the Basketball Hall of Fame in 2012. He also played for the USA Basketball Men's National Team and won a gold medal in the 1996 Olympics. In 2002, he won the USA Men's Basketball Athlete of the Year award. Many fans still consider Miller to be the best Pacers player of all time. After he retired from basketball, he became a sports announcer on television.

REGGIE MILLER STATS

Points	25,279
Rebounds	4,182
Assists	4,141
Three-Pointers	2,560

ALLEN IVERSON

At 6 feet (1.8 m) and 165 pounds (74.8 kg), Allen Iverson is one of the smallest shooting guards in NBA history. Iverson played 14 NBA seasons for four different teams between 1996 and 2010. He was the first overall pick in the 1996 NBA Draft and started his career with the Philadelphia 76ers. Iverson scored 30 points in his first NBA game and won the Rookie of the Year award that season.

Iverson was the NBA's top scorer in four different seasons. He ranked in the top 10 for total points in 11 of his 14 seasons. Iverson was the NBA's MVP in 2000–2001 and was an All-Star 11 times. After playing for the Denver Nuggets and the Detroit Pistons, Iverson returned to Philadelphia for his final season in 2009–2010. He had his highest-scoring game of the season against fellow shooting guard Kobe Bryant. Iverson's 1,983 steals are 14th all-time in the NBA, and his 2.2 steals per game rank ninth all-time.

ALLEN IVERSON STATS

Points		24,368
Rebounds		3,394
Assists		5,624
Three-Pointers		1,059

CLYDE DREXLER

Clyde Drexler played 15 NBA seasons, most of them with the Portland Trail Blazers. Drexler joined the Trail Blazers after only three college seasons at the University of Houston. Nicknamed the Glide, Drexler's smooth style made him appear to float in the air as he took a shot.

Drexler spent his final three seasons in the NBA with the Houston Rockets. He was part of Houston's 1995 NBA championship team. Drexler averaged 21.5 points, 9.5 rebounds, and 6.8 assists in the 1995 Finals. The 10-time NBA All-Star was also a member of USA Basketball's Dream Team that won the gold medal at the Olympics in 1992. He was a member of the NBA's 50th and 75th Anniversary teams honoring the league's top players. After Drexler retired, he returned to the University of Houston as a coach.

CLYDE DREXLER STATS

🏀	Points	22,195
🏀	Rebounds	6,677
🏀	Assists	6,125
🏀	Three-Pointers	827

JAMES HARDEN

Even though his career is not yet over, James Harden is already one of the best shooting guards in NBA history. The Oklahoma City Thunder picked Harden in the first round of the 2009 NBA Draft. He helped lead the team to the NBA Finals in 2012. That year, he was part of the USA

Basketball Men's National Team and won a gold medal at the Olympics in London, England.

Harden left the Thunder in 2012 and played more than eight seasons with the Houston Rockets. With Houston, he led the league in scoring three years in a row from 2017 to 2020. He won the NBA MVP award in 2018. Harden's nickname is the Beard for his eye-catching facial hair. Early in the 2023-2024 season, he joined the Los Angeles Clippers. He is one of only four players in NBA history with at least 23,000 career points and 6,500 career assists.

JAMES HARDEN STATS

Points	24,693
Rebounds	5,648
Assists	7,015
Three-Pointers	2,754

Stats are accurate through the 2022–2023 NBA season.

DWYANE WADE

Dwyane Wade wore number 3 on his jersey. One of his favorite players, fellow shooting guard Allen Iverson, also wore number 3. Wade played for the Miami Heat for most of his 16-year career. He was a 13-time NBA All-Star with the Heat. Wade is the Heat's all-time leader in points, assists, steals, shots made, and shots taken.

Wade was the NBA's top scorer in 2008–2009. In 2008, he was also part of the USA Basketball Men's National Team. Known as the Redeem Team, Wade and his teammates won the gold medal for the US for the first time since 2000. Wade helped lead Miami to three NBA championships before leaving to play for the Chicago Bulls and the Cleveland Cavaliers. He returned to Miami in 2018 to finish his career. After his retirement from playing in 2020, he began a sneaker brand called Way of Wade. He is also a co-owner of the Utah Jazz.

DWYANE WADE STATS

Points	23,165
Rebounds	4,933
Assists	5,701
Three-Pointers	549

KOBE BRYANT

Basketball came easily to Kobe Bryant. During his freshman year of high school, he played on his school's varsity team. He played all five positions and averaged more than 30 points per game in his junior year.

Bryant joined the Los Angeles Lakers in 1996 and played his entire 20-year career with the team. He won five NBA championships with the Lakers. He was a two-time NBA Finals MVP and an 18-time All-Star.

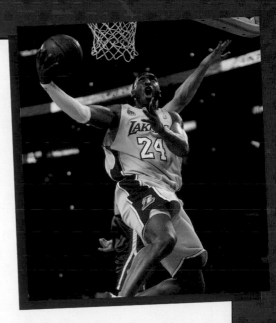

Bryant was an accurate outside shooter and was also skilled at slam-dunking. He led the NBA in total points four times and ranks fourth all-time for career points. Bryant is the only shooting guard to score at least 80 points in a game, and one of only eight players in NBA history to score at least 70 in one game.

The Lakers retired his jersey numbers in 2017 to honor his career. No Lakers players will wear numbers 8 and 24 again. Bryant also won an Academy Award in 2018 for his short film *Dear Basketball*. He became a member of the Basketball Hall of Fame in 2020 shortly after dying in a helicopter crash.

KOBE BRYANT STATS

Points	33,643
Rebounds	7,047
Assists	6,306
Three-Pointers	1,827

Many people consider Michael Jordan the greatest basketball player of all time. He is one of the most famous athletes in history and helped make basketball popular around the world. A well-known photo from 1984 shows Jordan leaping toward the basket. This image inspired the Air Jordan logo for Nike sports gear.

Jordan played most of his 15 NBA seasons with the Chicago Bulls. He won six NBA championships with the team. Jordan won five NBA MVP awards and six NBA Finals MVP awards. He led the NBA in total points 11 times and was a 14-time All-Star.

In 1993, Jordan retired from basketball after the death of his father. He played minor league baseball and rejoined the Bulls after missing one season. In 1998, he retired again before coming back to play two seasons for the Washington Wizards. Jordan was a member of USA Basketball's Men's National Team and won gold medals at the 1984 and 1992 Olympic Games. In 2022, the NBA renamed the league's MVP trophy after Jordan.

MICHAEL JORDAN STATS

	Points	32,292
	Rebounds	6,672
	Assists	5,633
	Three-Pointers	581

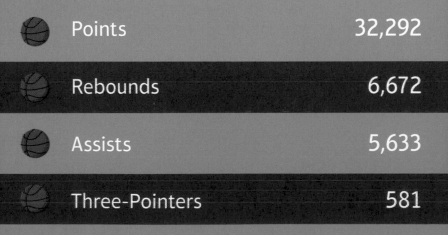

EVEN MORE G.O.A.T.

There have been so many amazing shooting guards in NBA history. Choosing only 10 is a challenge. Here are 10 others who could have made the G.O.A.T. list.

....

No. 11	TRACY MCGRADY
No. 12	GEORGE GERVIN
No. 13	MANU GINOBILI
No. 14	JERRY WEST
No. 15	VICKIE JOHNSON
No. 16	JOE JOHNSON
No. 17	JIMMY BUTLER
No. 18	SEIMONE AUGUSTUS
No. 19	SIDNEY MONCRIEF
No. 20	KATIE SMITH

YOUR G.O.A.T.

It's your turn to make a G.O.A.T. list about shooting guards. Start by doing research. Consider the rankings in this book. Then check out the Learn More section on page 31. Explore the books and websites to learn more about basketball players of the past and present.

You can search online for more information about great players too. Check with a librarian, who may have other resources for you. You might even try reaching out to basketball teams or players to see what they think.

Once you're ready, make your list of the greatest players of all time. Then ask people you know to make G.O.A.T. lists and compare them. Do you have players no one else listed? Are you missing anybody your friends think is important? Talk it over and try to convince them that your list is the G.O.A.T.!

GLOSSARY

assist: a pass from a teammate that leads directly to a score

conference: a group of teams. The NBA has two conferences, the Eastern Conference and the Western Conference.

draft: when teams take turns choosing new players

jump shot: a shot made by jumping into the air and releasing the ball with one or both hands at the peak of the jump

logo: a symbol used to advertise something

rebound: grabbing and controlling the ball after a missed shot

semifinal: a game or a series of games coming before the final round in a tournament

slam-dunk: to make a shot by jumping high into the air and throwing the ball down through the basket

steal: when a basketball player takes the ball from an opposing player

three-pointer: a shot taken from behind the three-point line on the court that counts for three points

LEARN MORE

Kortemeier, Todd, and Josh Anderson. *Inside the NBA Finals*. Parker, CO: The Child's World, 2023.

Levit, Joe. *Basketball's G.O.A.T.: Michael Jordan, LeBron James, and More*. Minneapolis: Lerner Publications, 2020.

Monson, James. *Behind the Scenes Basketball*. Minneapolis: Lerner Publications, 2020.

Official NBA Stats
https://www.nba.com/stats

Sports Illustrated Kids: Basketball
https://www.sikids.com/basketball

WNBA Stats
https://stats.wnba.com/

INDEX

PHOTO ACKNOWLEDGMENTS

Image credits: Maddie Meyer/Staff/Getty Images, p.4; Maddie Meyer/Staff/Getty Images, p.5; Thearon W. Henderson/Contributor/Getty Images, p.6; G Fiume/Contributor/Getty Images, p.7; Otto Greule Jr/Stringer/Getty Images, p.8; Kellie Landis/Staff/Getty Images, p.9; Christian Petersen/Staff/Getty Images, p.10; ANTONIO SCORZA/Staff/Getty Images, p.11; MediaNews Group/Boston Herald via Getty Images/Contributor/Getty Images, p.12; Elsa/Staff/Getty Images, p.13; G Fiume/Contributor/Getty Images, p.14; Focus On Sport/Contributor/Getty Images, p.15; The Sporting News/Contributor/Getty Images, p.16; G Fiume/Contributor/Getty Images, p.17; Focus On Sport/Contributor/Getty Images, p.18; Focus On Sport/Contributor/Getty Images, p.19; Mitchell Leff/Contributor/Getty Images, p.20; Andy Lyons/Staff/Getty Images, p.21; Jim McIsaac/Contributor/Getty Images, p.22; Rob Foldy/Contributor/Getty Images, 23; Lisa Blumenfeld/Contributor/Getty Images, p.24; Lisa Blumenfeld/Stringer/Getty Images, p.25; Mitchell Layton/Contributor/Getty Images, p.26; Jonathan Daniel/Stringer/Getty Images, p.27

Cover: Christian Petersen/Staff/Getty Images; Streeter Lecka/Staff/Getty Images; Stacy Revere/Contributor/Getty Images